THE FABULANARCHIST
LUXURY UPRISING

PRAISE FOR *THE FABULANARCHIST LUXURY UPRISING*

'Jack Houston is a one-off. His poems are surreally engaging, sending the reader into territory that seems eerily familiar but at the same time is completely destabilising. His world has a homespun simplicity about it, where things are themselves until they are transformed into something else. Facts may be otherwise, and yet we trust him, because it's clear through his form and music, his playful seriousness, that he's a poet who knows what he's doing. This is a debut brimming with delirious pleasures, a fabulanarchy indeed!'
Tamar Yoseloff

'In Jack Houston's world, a table can precisely be a table, so solid you could dine out on it. Then again, a wind-blown plastic bag can also be a ballerina and he can dress up as Captain Barnacles from *The Octonauts* – at his wife's request, of course. He can turn the reader into a dog. The seemingly 'domestic' and 'ordinary' are often little primed traps full of surprise. Deceptively casual and wrongfooting, in exactly the right way. Sniff it out. Lap it up.'
Matthew Caley

OTHER TITLES FROM THE EMMA PRESS

POETRY PAMPHLETS

how the first sparks became visible, by Simone Atangana Bekono, tr. from Dutch by David Colmer
do not be lulled by the dainty starlike blossom, by Rachael Matthews
With others in your absence, by Zosia Kuczyńska
Sandsnarl, by Jon Stone
This House, by Rehema Njambi
is, thinks Pearl, by Julia Bird
What the House Taught Us, by Anne Bailey
Overlap, by Valerie Bence
The Bell Tower, by Pamela Crowe
Ovarium, by Joanna Ingham
Milk Snake, by Toby Buckley

SHORT STORIES

The Secret Box, by Daina Tabūna, tr. from Latvian by Jayde Will
Tiny Moons: A year of eating in Shanghai, by Nina Mingya Powles
Postcard Stories 2, by Jan Carson
Hailman, by Leanne Radojkovich

BOOKS FOR CHILDREN

My Sneezes Are Perfect, by Rakhshan Rizwan
The Bee Is Not Afraid of Me: A Book of Insect Poems
Cloud Soup, by Kate Wakeling

ART SQUARES

Menagerie, by Cheryl Pearson, illustrated by Amy Evans
One day at the Taiwan Land Bank Dinosaur Museum, written and illustrated by Elīna Eihmane
Pilgrim, by Lisabelle Tay, illustrated by Reena Makwana
The Fox's Wedding, by Rebecca Hurst, illus. by Reena Makwana

THE FABULANARCHIST LUXURY UPRISING

POEMS BY JACK HOUSTON

THE EMMA PRESS

for M, A, K & E

☙

THE EMMA PRESS

First published in the UK in 2022 by The Emma Press Ltd.
Poems © Jack Houston 2022.

All rights reserved.

The right of Jack Houston to be identified as the author of this work has been asserted in accordance with the Copyright, Designs and Patents Act 1988.

ISBN 978-1-912915-96-5

A CIP catalogue record of this book
is available from the British Library.

Printed and bound in the UK by the Holodeck, Birmingham.

Cover design by Amy Louise Evans.

The Emma Press
theemmapress.com
hello@theemmapress.com
Birmingham, UK

CONTENTS

My New Table 1
An Economy of Insight 2
Ballet Lesson 3
boom 5
256 love poems 6
Rough Guide 10
And then he mentioned he was currently 'sleeping outside' 12
Ars Poetica 13
the pool is only *twelve steps* from the apartment! 14
A New Collective Noun for the Robin 16
Captain Barnacles 18
Utopia 20
precision munition 24
The Hope of Ever Being Found 25
Bonfires 27
Elegy for Myself 28

Acknowledgements 30
About the poet 30

My New Table

is large.
So large I can't quite see over it.

One expects tables to be about hip height.
Easy to rest a mug on.

Or sit at
to undertake an activity

such as eating.
Or drawing.

Or resting elbows
to make a sling with the palms,

face held
towards a convenient window.

This table can be walked under
with only the slightest stoop.

The wide space between its legs
easily swept. Easy to bring

the four chairs –
which are also large,

one for each side – close, to hide
underneath

in what I have discovered
is a remarkably comfortable place.

An Economy of Insight

There's a serious-sounding expert
on this morning's Radio 4
explaining the recent dips, thrusts, flips
and rushes of the stock market.

They're saying something about the end
of year, its concomitant verve and
re-adjustments, when over the airwaves
and into my kitchen: a clacking of claw.

This clack followed by a cluck,
the expert telling Martha Kearney
they've brought with them a hen.
A silence descends upon the studio

as the expert explains how here and now,
in the twenty-first century, the hen
will feel little distress as its throat is slit,
it being pre-fed anti-anxiety chickenfeed.

Next, blood tinkling onto metal bowl,
the sound of cutting into skin, flesh,
the schlooping of heart, spleen, liver
onto studio table. And as I wait

for the expert to finish digging around
in the now fully-expired chicken's viscera,
cup of tea held before my still-pursed lips,
I find myself hoping the signs are okay.

Ballet Lesson

A blue plastic bag twirls up to lift
and float on an updraft that began
with a flap of pigeonwing
somewhere on the outskirts of Xi'an,

an updraft that built slowly and then, in a seemingly
  organic fashion,
raced out over the Pacific,
its final destination
not yet specific

and anyway unknowable
to itself, it simply being a gasp of the heavens
and therefore completely unable
to sustain in its inexorable quest even

the illusion of agency toward something
either exciting or banal
as it now heads south to blow over the ocean funnelling
its way through the famous and Panamanian canal.

How one section of the wideness of our sky
can be considered separately from
any other I don't know, but as this breeze carries over the
  Caribbean Isles
it will not create any sort of storm,

will in no way accumulate to wipe out the homes
and small businesses,

the dreams and things bought on loan,
the very existences

of an entire island's inhabitants, but instead come here,
high outside my fifth-floor window, where it crumples and flexes
this blue plastic bag, pushing it through the air
into a twisting motion which is as expressive

as a ballerina
executing a perfect fouetté
as I sit and watch, concertinaed
into my settee,

the ballerina's arms stretching out, the ground
below them spinning on the pointe of their toes,
their other leg kicking them round
and around and around three more times in a row.

boom

are you experienced? said the man I said yes of course I am experienced and though it took a bit to get on once up I was off like a dog from a trap across the wide sea that lay ahead of me and the man's lad had to power alongside in his little speedboat and knock me from the windsurf board and drag me back and I said did you see that? I totally smashed it

256 love poems

a pick your own adventure

A I

The body of the world is like a potato.
See the way a straight line
drawn around its surface will always return
to the same potato place.

A II

Hippos, so closely related to cetaceans,
yet so unknowing of their whaleish history,
wade out into their muddy waters not fully
cognisant of the tails they've left behind.

A III

I climbed out, my ears full of suds, and dripped,
the floor receiving a small part of my bath.
I asked you to pass me the towel
with which I'd dry my sensitive crevices.

A IV

It was then that you mentioned the fruit salad
had wished its contents might come from tins.

B I

Aboard our small skiff with nothing
but the wind, the dark sky and the stars
to guide us, you told me to hold on to the rigging
as the boat rose and fell with each swell.

B II

We gathered round a pot of fresh-dug mud
and you buried a tomato, single, cherry.
I tapped down the dirt and a few weeks later
we were parents to too many tomato plants.

B III

I have mentioned I hope to be passionate,
and I've shown you I hope to be able.
I've promised I'll try to be balanced
like the legs on our dining room table.

B IV

Unclipping the plastic contraption from around my jaw,
I said, No, not like that. *Nuzz*le me.

C I

The situations I have known so well before.
The times I've bent to dustpan-brush the floor.
The only thing we'll ever want is more.
This is the only thing of which I'm sure.

C II

But absences of sound can lead to utterances
misconstrued, you said. I agreed, had to,
but couldn't feasibly have told you, then,
that this wasn't what I'd been trying to get at.

C III

If there were time to, I'd repeat this.
I'd say this again if I only had time.
If there were time to, I'd repeat this.
I'd say this again if I only had time.

C IV

Still, my hay fever was worse in the mornings.
You said, It's the trees, darling, making love.

D I

Our desire came pouring in through a hatch
in the ceiling like little pieces of Styrofoam
rising past our ankles, knees, and up to our bums.
We had to hope the roof window would open.

D II

Waiting for the making up there'd be running.
I knew this like a driver waiting at the station
for the passenger at Clapton who runs down
the stairs, shouting, Wait, wait! Hold on. Wait.

D III

We're abed, or almost, after a long evening
of tv and the odd sweet treat. We've already kissed
goodnight when you sit bolt upright, feel for the
light, and turning it on ask me, Is that it?

D IV

And though now finished I realise there might be
one or two more things I wish I'd thought to say.

Rough Guide

after Lucretius

Getting wherever this is has likely done you in,
adjusting to a new sun's swing,
so do try and get some sleep, if you can.
When you're set you can start to explore.

There'll be a range of languages to try and understand,
the odd new smell and food galore,
though I'm not sure we'll ever agree
on what *that's* supposed to be.

Some things will hang in the sky,
and some things will explode. You might ask why.
Some folk have a terrible time,
their luggage lost before they arrive,

left wondering how they'll ever survive
their stay, in what is frankly a dive.
Still, there are rules that must be obeyed.
One of these: be brave.

Or at least as brave as you feel.
Enjoy the mid-year bloom, the all-night raves, the ride
the only moon takes to fit perfectly over
the central star. The water's lovely

in a multiple-bathtub cascade.
And to soak in. I quite like bears.
But only in certain venues.
Faces. Smiles are in them. They crease. Then fade.

There now, don't cry. Time slides
here quicker than a swimming-pool flume,
but you've a wait now, before you're back in the air.
Perfect your tall tales of adventure

as a nice someone in a smart uniform smiles
and checks, oh, something essential.
Let yourself be lifted into the ozone.
Return to whatever it is you've come from.

And then he mentioned he was currently 'sleeping outside'
for T

Outside, as if in an open boat, each warm current
    lapping at the gunwales, sails
        tucked fast to the boom.

Outside, in the crackling air of the city,
    breathing the beneficent smog of our industries,
        of many more than a million cars.

Outside, where it's cool, wrapped up
    in the thick coat, the boots, the sleeping bag;
        like an infant, swaddled.

Outside and free to awake when he wants to,
    to stretch and stand up and move onward
        not held by house or home.

Outside, and every bright star of the galaxy
    a pinprick of paradise
        welcoming him to the night.

Ars Poetica

Free entry.

Free wine.

the pool is only twelve steps from the apartment!

everybody loves the diving in bit

                                                                                          the leap

through air   with a whoop   arms raised   in celebration
a breath-held expectation

                                                      of the splash to come

and once under

                                           I'm deep in the same wet struggle
to keep myself above the surface   not slip be-
low

      yet here I am

                    standing at the edge

                                                               toes curl-
ing over the lip

                                          staring down into the slip-slap of these weeny waves

                                                and though I know I'll la-

ter hate the water

                      in my hair

                                    its drip-dripping

behind my ears and flowing

                                  down my spine to soak

a lonely-sodden print of bum

                                          on towels laid out

                                  I'm only gonna go and dive on in again

A New Collective Noun for the Robin

Few of us are aware that robins live life largely underground,
flitting through the robin-sized tunnels that connect
the nests in which they parent their eggs to the hidey-
holes from which they occasionally appear.
And the two of us had only just begun to explain

to the leaves of St Peter's how excited we were
– you in your new suit, me in red as well –
when the forest-floor split open and an inferno
of robins flew up and engulfed us, grappling
with their tiny claws to pull us skyward.

We quickly got used to life on the wing,
able to envisage so much more from height,
the exhilaration of toes skipping tree-tops,
sleeping high as kites and blackbirds and the wrens
that would soon become our friends.

We even managed to make love in the cumulonimbus.
The robins didn't seem to mind. Our first child burst forth
exuberant, but the robins did not falter, kept their grip,
held the three of us as a few flew down to stitch the damage,
and as the next two slipped out blue as evening, still

as puddles, they fluttered tight to rub the breath back in.
They know so much of wing-strain and feather over-flap,
the robins, but not once have they ever complained,
the time they've spent pressed in with everything buried
filling them with a strange and subterranean energy

I hope will hold all five of us in flight.

Captain Barnacles

My wife wishes me to dress as Captain Barnacles
in bed. Yes, that's correct, Captain Barnacles,
from the animated CBeebies programme, *The Octonauts*.
When I say 'in bed' I'm using that phrase euphemistically,
as in, embarking upon an attempt at sexual congress,
not simply sleeping in Captain Barnacles-themed pyjamas.

She wants me to do the voice, as well.
If you're not sure who Captain Barnacles is
(with our two little tykes, we're well acquainted),
he is a talking polar bear in a military-style uniform
complete with a little blue captain's hat.
I'm not sure where she gets her ideas from.

She tells me it's the least I can do.
I wait for her to go out. I want this first time
to be private. Sourcing a navy-blue onesie
with a light blue collar has proved difficult,
so I've had to sew one myself; but with this blue belt
and boots (both matching the collar), I should look the part.

And what a part. My chest fills and back straightens
at the sight of myself, uniformed and bear-like.
I begin to feel the saltwater of the world's oceans
calling me, the wind above the waves telling me
to sail out toward the far horizons of adventure,
the character of Captain Barnacles filling me

with a sense of purpose, a sense of what is right,
a new affinity for the creatures of the deep.
We're going to have to have a serious talk
when she gets home; I've never felt so liberated.
I can't help feel that this is whom I'm meant to be.
Never in my life have I ever felt so free.

Utopia

for my little soldiers

In the year 2121,
we're all now too aware that a sofa is simply a bench
constructed from the hewn corpse
of a tree, covered in a mesh made from the amniotic fibres
of oppressedly mono-cropped cotton plants
& filled with the plumage
from many a murdered full-grown duck,

but, to keep this re-enactment faithful,
the woman has to sit on one
to breastfeed her baby.

It is a baby she has birthed herself.

In our spark-bright, fusion-fuelled & post-chore future,
many choose to perform as we had to before:
the over-intimate messiness of a copulative conception,
the aches & the strains of an internal gestation,
a hypnobirth in a tepid paddling pool.

At a desk in the same room sits the raw-biological father of
    the infant.
This young family share the living space:
a structure comprised of four small yet interconnected boxes.
He is currently composing a piece of verbal art
on a binary-processing interface device
whilst one of the other children – & believe it or not, they
    have three –

reaches up to grab the roller-pointer
on the table, a device our ancestors
once commonly referred to as a 'mouse'.

The man says *Stop that*
with rather more annoyance
than seems strictly necessary,
as the woman stands,
swings the baby onto her hip
& reminds him it is his day to work.

& yes, they both work,
both surrendering time
to receive a payment worthless outside the confines of this fantasyland
they & so many others
insist upon creating: she,
sitting & listening to her fellow artists
in a facsimile of the antique practice of 'psychodynamic counselling',
while he labours in a building
our forebears would have called 'the local library'.

Here, he will 'shelve' books,
'help' 'service users' 'use'
the self-service issuing machines
& even 'chat' to a{n elderly} lady
about her {implanted varicose} veins.

The entire building,
the entire locale, in fact,
fashioned so this simulacrum of an era
can feel as accurate as possible.

Indeed, no detail is deemed too small:
the nearby pond & its gene|membered ducks,
tarmacadam roadways & fractional distillate of petroleum
    fuel-oil powered buses,
the water recycling systems & brick-built educational &
    medical institutions of the day;

the man is even going to,
at one point this very afternoon,
'read a story', vocally(!),
to a group of fellow child-actors aged five or under.

But now,
returning from the room that our progenitors knew as
    'the kitchen', he comes
holding two plates: & yes,
as shocking as this may seem to us today,
instead of anally suppositing their carbohydrates
inhibited by an amino acid & lipid complex
like normal people, they will eat this breakfast.
Using their mouths.

The abode, you will have noticed,
is bizarrely small,
since the Fabulanarchist Luxury Uprising
of the years 2042/4/6/8

people have lived in buildings the size,
shape, decoration & location of their choosing, but here
this family of five
live in a two-bedroomed dwelling
in an area once known as 'The London Borough of Hackney.'

However, I think we can forgive them this penchant for the historical.
These young people are, after all,
only trying to make something more
than just another Wonderful Work of Art,
to hark back to when it was still possible to erupt upon the world,
to make something rotten something new.

When you, too, could grow up to become a hero of the revolution,

or maybe play one of their parents.

precision munition

they're sharing their toys when you see
a glint in the bigger one's eyes like the sun

come off the slip-slap swell of a wide ocean
the aircraft carrier floating serene

through gunmetal waters the ground crew
fussing at great speed to ready the jet

strapping the pilot into his flight suit
pumping five thousand litres of fuel

loading & priming precision munitions
& those back home not fully aware

there has already been a decision
for their once peaceful people to war

& one of their own is to be lofted to prove
their power while they only want to be loved

The Hope of Ever Being Found

I want us to try and imagine you are this
bright-eyed exhibit of dogness:

                         wire-haired and young, Yorkie-ish,
                               with a stubby tail
         wildly exhibiting a most vigorous waggling
as you skitter-scurry snuffle at the trouser-legs
of everyone who passes
             and up to a woman who is eating a sandwich
                                       on a bench.

Using the medium of whine and eye-and-ear strain
you try and communicate
both the fact of your lostness
and that you wouldn't say no to a bit of that sandwich.

                  I am the person you've just run up to.
                     I'm sitting on a bench
                     as a scruffy puppy comes a-yapping
                        and eyeing my sandwich.
I reach down to lift the little disc
attached to the dog's collar. There's no number,
just a blank.
             I search the faces of the people around us.
           None of them seem to be missing a small dog.

You watch my search
and the fact I've not taken a bite
of my lunch for nearly two whole minutes,

a scandalous lack of concern
> for what you can clearly smell is a cheese ploughman's,
>> as another dog, a Staffie, saunters over
>>> and sits down.

You are now two dogs,
both gazing up at me expectantly.

> Your second you stretches front paws forward,
> pushes bum to sky and you no longer feel any need
>> to exist outside of this poem

as the two of you tumble over each other
to roll round on floor. And here's more dogs,
and more, all barking and lolloping, bounding around
> and weeing up the trees,
> scratching at the fleas behind their ears.

Bonfires

It's rare now, beech. Takes at least three years
to season. But he's like that, my neighbour,
Peter Cooper. Always has to possess the best
of everything. I should listen to Susan,

shouldn't let it get to me, shouldn't build ours
any higher. I ask her if she wants to light it,
but she says she's happy to just hold the rope,
so I go and round up the kids. Harriet, eldest, first,

cautiously approaches the bars. No amount
of gentle entreaty will convince her
she's quite safe. And then Noah, dear sweet, Noah.
He'll follow that sister of his anywhere.

A quick dash of petrol and we're off,
the flames catching the kindling in the middle,
starting to lick up the outside lengths
of what is still only pine. And of course

Harriet starts up with her piteous squeal;
Noah with his cough. I peer across the gardens
and there's Peter, waving and smiling,
his wife holding their cage over their bonfire,

the calm faces of his two aglow above the flames.

Elegy for Myself

At a point as high as the lowest rib
of a tall man, perhaps heart-height
on someone smaller, the tree trunk's cut,
its branches, limbs carried off.

Levelled by chainsaw,
the honey-gold circumference of its centre
now the smooth top of an organic monolith
set by the side of a path in the park.

Walking past, I realise I don't remember
there being a tree there.

ACKNOWLEDGEMENTS

I'm grateful to the editors of the following publications where some of these poems first appeared: *Finished Creatures, New Boots and Pantisocracies, Orbis, Perverse, The Rialto, Rupture, Stand* and *Welling Up: Poetry on Human Rights and the Environment* (Palewell Press).

'A New Collective Noun for the Robin' was highly commended in the 2019 Waltham Forest Poetry Competition. 'Captain Barnacles' was shortlisted for the 2018 Keats-Shelley Prize.

I'm indebted to Forest Poets, The Hackney Libraries Lockdown Poetry Workshop, and my fellow Poetry School MA students whose keen eyes, kind ears and intelligent comments helped make these poems into those you have just finished reading.

Thanks also to Hackney Council whose award of Housing Benefit greatly assisted in the completion of this manuscript.

ABOUT THE POET

Jack Houston is a writer and public librarian from London. His poetry has been shortlisted for the 2017 Basil Bunting and 2018 Keats-Shelley Prizes, and has appeared in publications including *Blackbox Manifold, Magma, The Morning Star, The Rialto, Poetry London* and *Stand*. His short fiction was shortlisted for the 2020 Brick Lane Bookshop Prize and the 2020 BBC National Short Story Award. He lives in Hackney with his partner and their three children, two goldfish and a stick insect.